Stark County District Library
www.StarkLibrary.org
330.452.0665

Y0-CJG-682

MAY -- 2019

NATURAL MARVELS

Fabled Waters

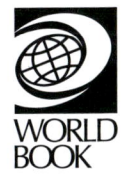

WORLD BOOK

World Book, Inc.
180 North LaSalle Street, Suite 900
Chicago, Illinois 60601
USA

For information about other World Book publications, please visit our website at www.worldbook.com or call 1-800-WORLDBK (967-5325).

For information about sales to schools and libraries, please call 1-800-975-3250 (United States) or 1-800-837-5365 (Canada).

© 2017 World Book, Inc. All rights reserved. This volume may not be reproduced in whole or in part in any form without prior written permission from the publisher. WORLD BOOK and the GLOBE DEVICE are registered trademarks or trademarks of World Book, Inc.

Library of Congress Cataloging-in-Publication Data

Title: Fabled waters.
Description: Chicago, Illinois: World Book, Inc., a Scott Fetzer Company, [2017] | Series: Natural marvels | Includes index.
Identifiers: LCCN 2016048006 | ISBN 9780716633693
Subjects: LCSH: Water--Juvenile literature. | Bodies of water--Juvenile literature. | Ganges River Delta (Bangladesh and India)--Juvenile literature. | Great Lakes (North America)--Juvenile literature. | Niagara Falls (N.Y. and Ont.)--Juvenile literature.
Classification: LCC GB662.3 .F33 2017 | DDC 551.48--dc23
LC record available at https://lccn.loc.gov/2016048006

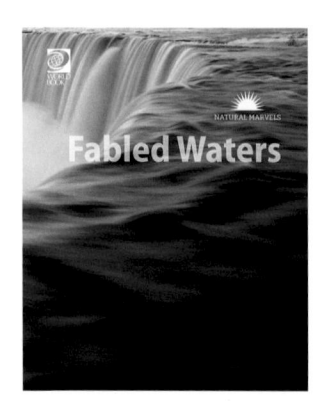

Over eons, the forces of nature have sculpted Earth in certain locations to create majestic landscapes of great beauty. Some of the most spectacular landforms are featured in this series of books. This image shows Niagara Falls in Ontario, Canada.

This edition:
ISBN: 978-0-7166-3369-3 (hc.)
ISBN: 978-0-7166-3363-1 (set, hc.)

Also available as:
ISBN: 978-0-7166-3378-5 (e-book, EPUB3)

Printed in China by Shenzhen Wing King Tong Paper Products Co., Ltd. Shenzhen, Guangdong
1st printing March 2017

STAFF

Writer: Jeff De La Rosa

Executive Committee

President
Jim O'Rourke

Vice President and Editor in Chief
Paul A. Kobasa

Vice President, Finance
Donald D. Keller

Vice President, Marketing
Jean Lin

Vice President, International Sales
Maksim Rutenberg

Director, Human Resources
Bev Ecker

Editorial

Director, Digital and Print Content Development
Emily Kline

Editor, Digital and Print Content Development
Kendra Muntz

Manager, Science
Jeff De La Rosa

Editors, Science
William D. Adams
Nicholas V. Kilzer

Administrative Assistant, Digital and Print Content Development
Ethel Matthews

Manager, Contracts & Compliance (Rights & Permissions)
Loranne K. Shields

Manager, Indexing Services
David Pofelski

Graphics and Design

Senior Art Director
Tom Evans

Senior Designer
Don Di Sante

Media Editor
Rosalia Bledsoe

Senior Cartographer
John M. Rejba

Manufacturing/Production

Production/Technology Manager
Anne Fritzinger

Proofreader
Nathalie Strassheim

Table of Contents

Introduction 4

Ganges 6

Where Is the Ganges and What's
Special About It?. 8

The Legend of Ma Ganga 10

Geography 12

How the Ganges Formed 14

Sacred River 16

Wildlife 18

Great Lakes 20

Where Are the Great Lakes and What's
Special About Them? 22

How the Great Lakes Formed. 24

Importance 26

Niagara Falls. 28

Where Is Niagara Falls
and What's Special About It? 30

How Niagara Falls Formed 32

Niagara Falls Attractions 34

Tourism 36

Glossary 38

Find Out More. 39

Index 40

Glossary There is a glossary of terms on page 38. Terms defined in the glossary are in type **that looks like this** on their first appearance on any spread (two facing pages). Words that are difficult to say are followed by a pronunciation (*pruh NUHN see AY shuhn*) the first time they are used.

Introduction

More than two-thirds of Earth's surface is covered in water. But most of this water is the salt water that fills Earth's oceans. Only three percent of Earth's water is fresh water. People need this water for drinking and watering crops. Since prehistoric times, the need for water has drawn human beings to the planet's lakes, ponds, rivers, and streams.

As these waters have sustained us, they have also inspired us. People stand in awe at the beauty of a towering waterfall or the destructive fury of a river at flood. This volume features three marvels of water that have inspired tales of awe and majesty in both ancient and modern people.

The Ganges (*GAN jeez*) has been called the world's most **sacred** river. It flows across northern India, from the slopes of the **Himalaya** to the Bay of Bengal. Each year, millions of pilgrims journey to bathe in the river and to take some of its water.

The Great Lakes, on the border between Canada and the United States, form the world's largest continuous body of fresh water. Together, Lake Huron, Lake Ontario, Lake Michigan, Lake Erie, and Lake Superior hold almost one-fifth of the fresh water on Earth's surface.

Niagara Falls, between Lake Erie and Lake Ontario, is among the world's most celebrated waterfall systems. Millions of people visit the falls each year to see the river thunder into the **basin** below.

Arctic Ocean
THE GREAT LAKES
North America
NIAGARA FALLS
Europe
Asia
GANGES RIVER
Africa
Pacific Ocean
Atlantic Ocean
Equator
South America
Indian Ocean
Australia
Pacific Ocean
Southern Ocean
Antarctica

A landform is a natural feature on Earth's surface, such as a mountain, river, or valley. This series of books, *Natural Marvels,* aims to explain how Earth's features formed over time. Some landforms—certain volcanoes, for example—can form over the course of a short time period. But, landforms usually take thousands or even millions of years to form. In these books, you will learn how forces on Earth, often over long time periods, can create landscapes of great beauty.

Ganges

7

Where Is the Ganges and What's Special About It?

The Ganges is India's greatest **waterway** and one of its longest rivers. Only the Indus and Brahmaputra rivers are longer in India. The Ganges runs about 1,560 miles (2,510 kilometers) across northern India, from the slopes of the **Himalaya,** the world's tallest mountains, to the Bay of Bengal.

The river is an important trade area. Its valley is fertile and densely populated. Some of India's largest cities, such as Kolkata and Kanpur, stand on the banks of the Ganges.

The Ganges is most important for the part it plays in the Hindu religion. Hindus consider it the most **sacred** river in India. Each year, thousands of Hindu pilgrims visit the Ganges to bathe in the river and to take home some of its water.

Some pilgrims come seeking to cleanse and purify themselves. The sick and crippled hope that the touch of the water will cure their ailments. Others come to place their dead in the river, which is said to release the soul from the cycle of death and *reincarnation* (rebirth of the soul in a new body).

The Ganges in northern India is surrounded by scenic and fertile valleys that support large populations.

9

The Legend of Ma Ganga

In the Hindu religion, the Ganges is personified by the goddess Ganga. Both she and the river itself are sometimes called *Ma Ganga,* which means *Mother Ganges.* The story of the river's origin involves three major of gods of Hinduism: (1) Brahma, the Creator; (2) Vishnu, the Preserver; and (3) Shiva, the Transformer.

According to Hindu beliefs, the Ganges was created by an *incarnation* (form) of Vishnu. Vishnu's incarnation stretched out his foot to measure the heavens. The nail of his big toe poked a hole in the heavens' edge, allowing the *divine* (holy) water beyond to rush through. The **sacred** waters flowed over the foot of Vishnu's incarnation and poured through the heavens, forming the Ganges.

At first, the Ganges was strictly a heavenly river. Its waters were brought to Earth by the descendants of King Sagara. According to **myth,** Sagara had 60,000 sons. When they died, their spirits were trapped on Earth. Sagara's sons begged Brahma to bring the Ganges to Earth, cleansing the spirits of the king's dead sons.

Brahma agreed, but Ganga was insulted. She decided to flood the Earth, killing everyone. Shiva stepped in, placing his head beneath the waters. Filtered through his hair, the waters of the Ganges flowed calmly to Earth.

A Hindu monk prays near the banks of the Ganges in the holy city of Varanasi in northern India.

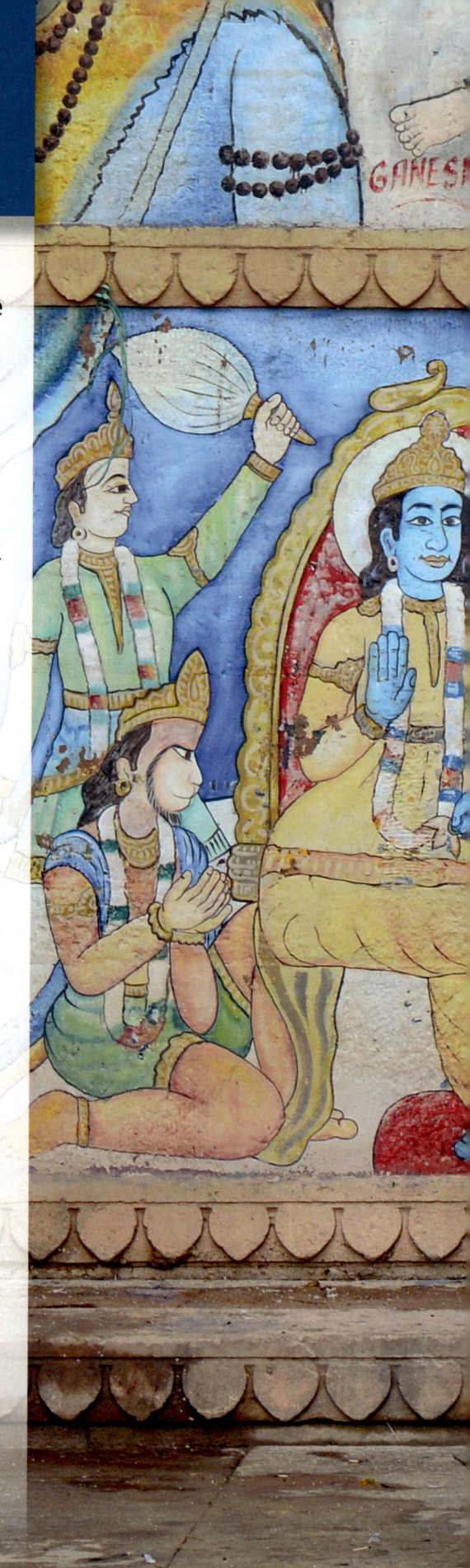

THE NILE

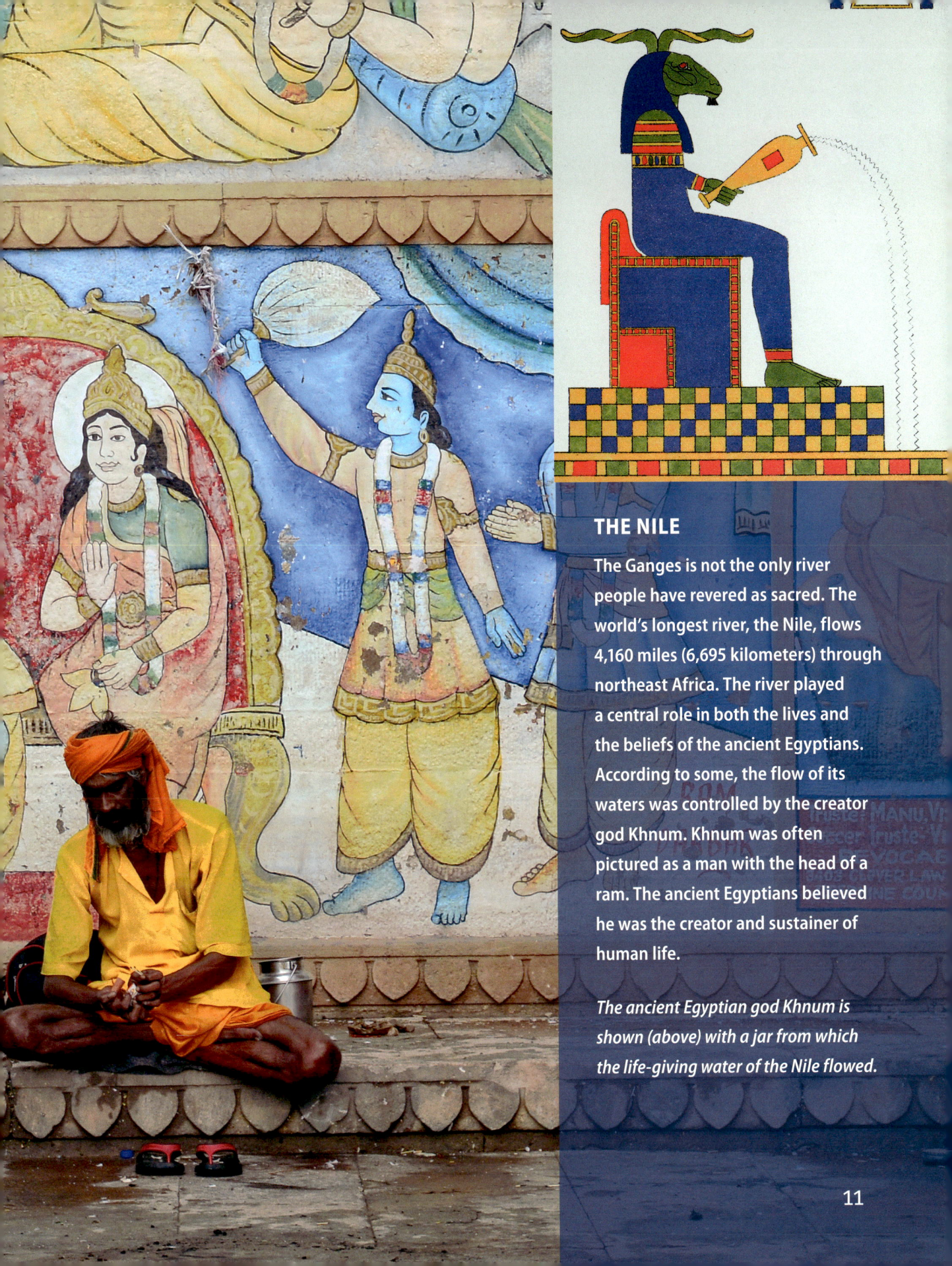

The Ganges is not the only river people have revered as sacred. The world's longest river, the Nile, flows 4,160 miles (6,695 kilometers) through northeast Africa. The river played a central role in both the lives and the beliefs of the ancient Egyptians. According to some, the flow of its waters was controlled by the creator god Khnum. Khnum was often pictured as a man with the head of a ram. The ancient Egyptians believed he was the creator and sustainer of human life.

The ancient Egyptian god Khnum is shown (above) with a jar from which the life-giving water of the Nile flowed.

Geography

The Ganges begins in the remote slopes of the **Himalaya,** the world's tallest mountains. There, water melting from the Gangotri **Glacier** flows from an ice cave more than 10,000 feet (3,000 meters) above sea level. This cave is known as Gaumakh, the cow's mouth. The water that flows from it is joined by other streams as it moves south through the Himalaya.

The Ganges veers east as it joins the Ramganga and Yamuna rivers. As the Ganges flows across northern India, it continues to be fed by other rivers and streams that flow into it, called **tributaries.** Together, the Ganges and its tributaries drain a vast, fertile region known as the Ganges river **basin.**

As it flows to the sea, the Ganges passes through dozens of major cities and many more small towns. The people who live in these areas rely on water from the Ganges for daily use and to water their crops. Eight percent of the world's population lives in the Ganges river basin.

Eventually, the Ganges passes into Bangladesh, where it is known as the Padma. The Padma joins with the Brahmaputra River. Where the combined rivers approach the ocean, they have deposited a vast plain of sediment called a **delta.** The Ganges Delta is a fertile wetland region.

Hindu pilgrims make their way to Gangotri Glacier, the source of the Ganges in the Himalaya mountain range.

THE YANGTZE RIVER

The Ganges river basin is the world's most populous river basin, but not by much. In China, about 6 percent of the world's population lives in the basin of the Yangtze River. The Yangtze River originates in the Tanggula Mountains of Qinghai Province, about 16,000 feet (4,880 meters) above sea level. It follows an irregular 3,900-mile (6,275-kilometer) course to the East China Sea. Thousands of Chinese live on the Yangtze River, aboard sailing craft called *junks*.

A junk (above) sails down the Yangtze river in China.

How the Ganges Formed

Earth's solid outer surface, or crust, is made up of vast rigid slabs of rock called **tectonic plates.** These plates slowly move over the hot, soft rock below, and the continents move with them. The plates spread apart, grind past one another, and sometimes collide.

India was once a huge island. About 50 million years ago, the motion of the plates caused it to collide with the rest of Asia. This collision raised up the **Himalaya.** It also led to the formation of a low-lying area at their feet called the Gangetic **basin.**

The Gangetic basin is watered by melting snow from the Himalaya and by heavy rains brought by seasonal winds called *monsoons.* All of that water has to go somewhere. Over time, a system of rivers formed draining the basin into the Bay of Bengal.

Nobody knows exactly when the Ganges formed. The river has probably flowed near its present course for tens of thousands of years.

The Ganges and its **tributaries** carry mineral-rich water down from the mountains. Over time, flooding has deposited much of these minerals on land, creating the fertile soils of the Gangetic basin. Mineral-rich silt from these soils also drains back into the Ganges. As the river's waters approach the sea, they slow. The silt drops out, forming the Ganges **Delta.**

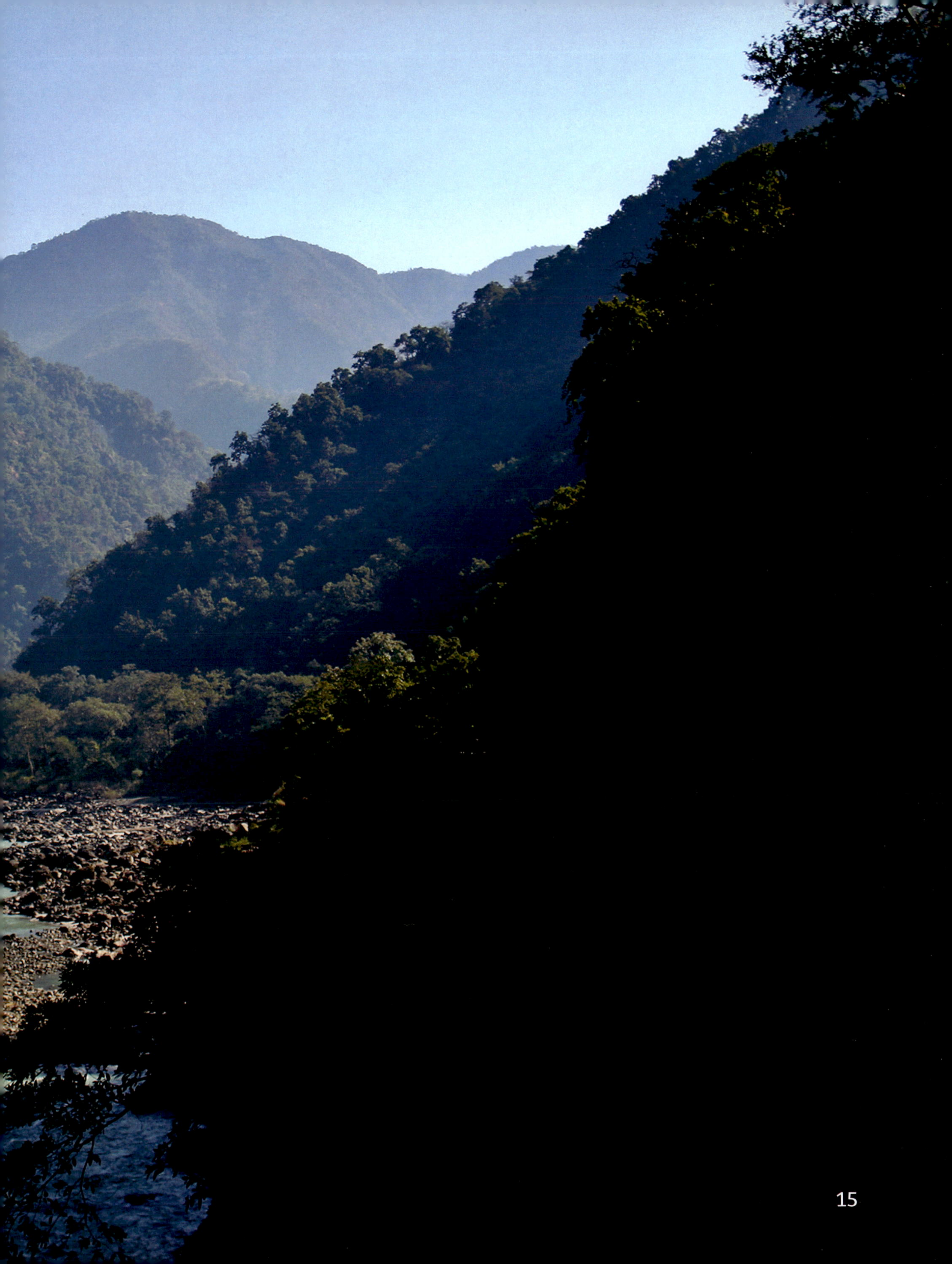

Sacred River

The Ganges plays a central role in Hindu spiritual life. Each year, millions of pilgrims travel to bathe in the river and to take home some water, which is thought to have cleansing powers. In towns and cities, the banks of the Ganges are dotted with temples and with *ghats*, stairways and platforms leading to the river's edge.

The Ganges is particularly celebrated in such holy cities as Allahabad, Haridwar, Rishikesh, and Varanasi. In such places, the river is daily honored in rituals called *aarti*. In these ceremonies, the river is offered light from burning wicks dipped in *ghee* (clarified butter). The offering may be accompanied by songs, speeches, and other celebrations.

Varanasi is India's holiest city. It is said that dying in Varanasi can bring *moksha*, release from the cycle, or repeating pattern, of death and rebirth. For this reason, many people come to Varanasi to die or to send off their dead. Each day in Varanasi, hundreds of bodies are cremated on ghats, their ashes swept into the Ganges.

About every third year, a giant festival called a Kumbh Mela is held at one of several **sacred** spots along the Ganges. At a Kumbh Mela, millions of pilgrims may bathe in the Ganges in a single day.

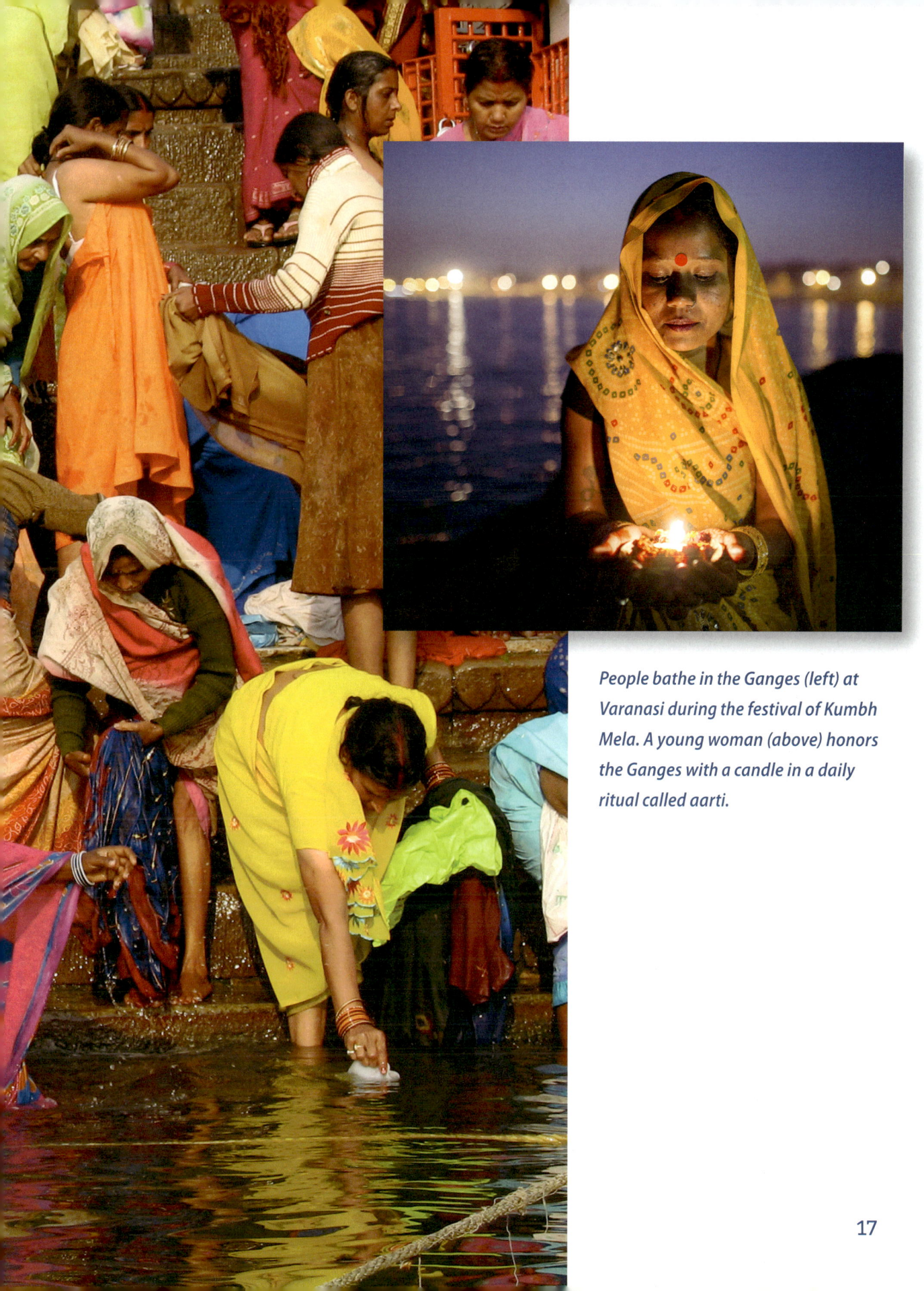

People bathe in the Ganges (left) at Varanasi during the festival of Kumbh Mela. A young woman (above) honors the Ganges with a candle in a daily ritual called aarti.

Wildlife

Despite the heavy **pollution**, many animals live in or near the Ganges and its **tributaries.** The river hosts India's greatest diversity of freshwater fish along with a number of amphibians and other water-living species. A variety of birds live and feed along the Ganges.

Much wildlife can be found in the river's less polluted upper regions. Rare and endangered snow leopards prowl the **Himalaya** where the Ganges begins. Above Kanpur, the Ganges is home to many ducks, wading birds, and gavials, crocodile relatives known for their extremely long, thin snouts. Elephants, jackals, and a type of deer called barasingha are a few of the animals that may be spotted along the river's banks.

A gavial (above) uses its long, thin snout to catch fish in the Ganges, while a barasingha deer (below) pauses to drink near the river edge.

Perhaps the best-known resident of the Ganges is the endangered Ganges river dolphin. This freshwater dolphin is also called the *susu* for the sucking noise it makes when it surfaces to breathe. The waters of the Ganges are also home to a rare freshwater shark, the critically endangered Ganges shark.

A swampy area of the Ganges **Delta** called the Sundarbans is home to the world's largest mangrove forest. The area is home to a wide variety of wildlife, including chital deer, crocodiles, king cobras, rhesus monkeys, lizards called water monitors, and the rare Bengal tiger.

A rare freshwater Ganges river dolphin (above) breaks the surface of the Ganges. Rhesus monkeys (below) are common in the mangrove forests of the Ganges Delta.

Great Lakes

21

Where Are the Great Lakes and What's Special About Them?

Fresh water is rare on Earth's surface. Yet a full 18 percent of Earth's surface fresh water can be found in one place: the aptly named Great Lakes. These five vast lakes form a large portion of the border between the United States and Canada, in east-central North America.

Lake Superior is the westernmost of the Great Lakes and the largest. It has the largest surface of any of freshwater lake in the world, measuring about 350 miles (560 kilometers) from east to west and 160 miles (260 kilometers) north to south. Lake Superior has an average depth of nearly 500 feet (170 meters) and is 1,330 feet (405 meters) deep at its deepest point. The second largest Great Lake, Lake Michigan, is the only one of the five lakes that lies entirely within the United States. Lake Michigan is connected to the third largest lake, Lake Huron, at the Straits of Mackinac (*MAK uh NAW*). Lake Erie has the smallest *volume* (space) of the Great Lakes. Its surface measures about a third that of Lake Superior. Lake Ontario, the easternmost lake, is slightly smaller than Lake Erie in surface area but much deeper.

Together, the Great Lakes make up the largest freshwater lake system in the world. They have a combined surface area of 94,200 square miles (244,200 square kilometers). Spread evenly over an area the size of the United States, the water they hold would measure nearly 10 feet (3 meters deep).

Wind-swept waves on Lake Michigan, one of the five Great Lakes of North America which make up a large portion of the border between Canada and the United States

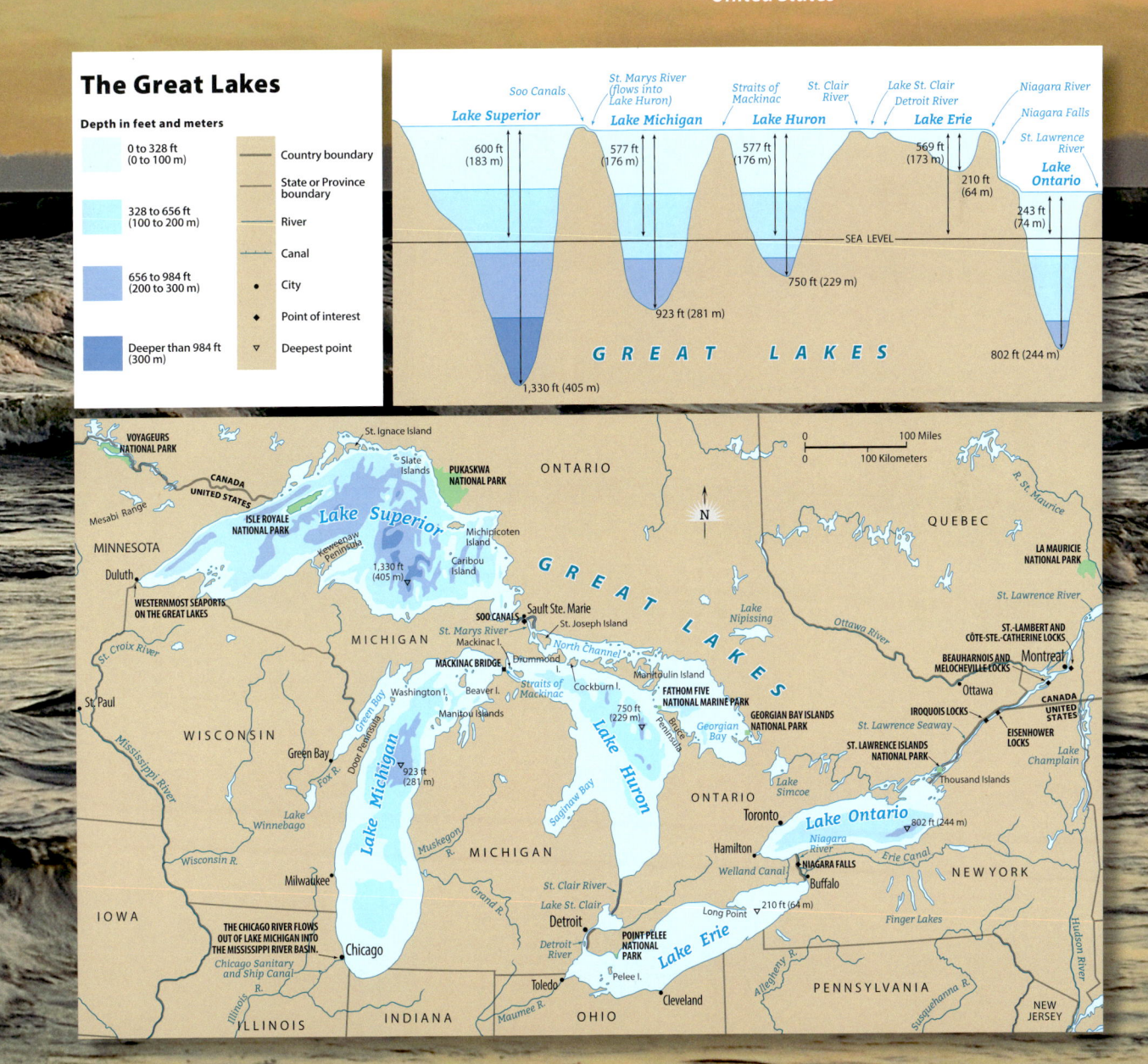

The Great Lakes

Depth in feet and meters

- 0 to 328 ft (0 to 100 m)
- 328 to 656 ft (100 to 200 m)
- 656 to 984 ft (200 to 300 m)
- Deeper than 984 ft (300 m)

- Country boundary
- State or Province boundary
- River
- Canal
- • City
- ♦ Point of interest
- ▽ Deepest point

Cross-section

Lake Superior	Lake Michigan	Lake Huron	Lake Erie	Lake Ontario
Soo Canals	St. Marys River (flows into Lake Huron)	Straits of Mackinac	St. Clair River / Detroit River	Niagara River / Niagara Falls / St. Lawrence River
600 ft (183 m)	577 ft (176 m)	577 ft (176 m)	569 ft (173 m)	210 ft (64 m) / 243 ft (74 m)
1,330 ft (405 m)	923 ft (281 m)	750 ft (229 m)		802 ft (244 m)

SEA LEVEL

GREAT LAKES

Map features

- Voyageurs National Park
- St. Ignace Island
- Slate Islands
- Pukaskwa National Park
- ONTARIO
- CANADA / UNITED STATES
- Mesabi Range
- Isle Royale National Park
- Lake Superior
- Keweenaw Peninsula
- Michipicoten Island
- Caribou Island
- MINNESOTA
- Duluth
- Westernmost seaports on the Great Lakes
- 1,330 ft (405 m)
- GREAT LAKES
- QUEBEC
- R. St. Maurice
- La Mauricie National Park
- St. Lawrence River
- St. Croix River
- MICHIGAN
- Sault Ste. Marie
- Soo Canals
- St. Joseph Island
- St. Marys River
- Mackinac I.
- Drummond
- North Channel
- Lake Nipissing
- Ottawa River
- St.-Lambert and Côte-Ste.-Catherine Locks
- Beauharnois and Melocheville Locks
- Montreal
- Ottawa
- St. Paul
- Mackinac Bridge
- Washington I.
- Beaver I.
- Straits of Mackinac
- Cockburn I.
- Manitoulin Island
- Fathom Five National Marine Park
- Bruce Peninsula
- Georgian Bay Islands National Park
- Georgian Bay
- St. Lawrence Seaway
- Iroquois Locks
- CANADA / UNITED STATES
- Eisenhower Locks
- Lake Champlain
- WISCONSIN
- Green Bay
- Door Peninsula
- Manitou Islands
- Fox R.
- 923 ft (281 m)
- 750 ft (229 m)
- St. Lawrence Islands National Park
- Thousand Islands
- Lake Winnebago
- Lake Michigan
- Saginaw Bay
- Lake Huron
- Lake Simcoe
- ONTARIO
- Toronto
- Lake Ontario
- 802 ft (244 m)
- Wisconsin R.
- Muskegon R.
- Hamilton
- Niagara River
- Erie Canal
- Milwaukee
- MICHIGAN
- Grand R.
- Welland Canal
- Niagara Falls
- Buffalo
- NEW YORK
- IOWA
- St. Clair River
- Lake St. Clair
- Long Point
- 210 ft (64 m)
- Finger Lakes
- THE CHICAGO RIVER FLOWS OUT OF LAKE MICHIGAN INTO THE MISSISSIPPI RIVER BASIN.
- Chicago
- Detroit
- Point Pelee National Park
- Lake Erie
- Chicago Sanitary and Ship Canal
- Detroit River
- Pelee I.
- Mississippi River
- ILLINOIS
- INDIANA
- Toledo
- Maumee R.
- OHIO
- Cleveland
- Allegheny R.
- PENNSYLVANIA
- Susquehanna R.
- Hudson River
- NEW JERSEY

Scale: 100 Miles / 100 Kilometers

23

How the Great Lakes Formed

Much of the landscape of northern North America has been carved by **glaciers**. A glacier is a huge mass of flowing ice. As glaciers move over the land, they grind and scour away at the ground beneath.

Over the last 2 million years, glaciers have repeatedly advanced, or pushed forward, south over the land where the Great Lakes are now found. At times, the glaciers reached about 6,600 feet (2,000 meters) thick. As the glaciers advanced, the heavy ice dug deep hollows in the ground. They also picked up and carried along great amounts of dirt and rocks.

The last advance of these glaciers took place about 25,000 years ago. The glaciers melted and withdrew, or pulled back, about 11,000 to 15,000 years ago. The melting ice deposited dirt and rocks, blocking the natural drainage of the deep hollows, or depressions, the glaciers had carved. Over time, the depressions filled with water, forming thousands of lakes, including the Great Lakes.

Waves crash on the shore of Lake Superior at Agawa Bay, Ontario. The huge lake is a lasting remnant of glaciers that once covered the land.

LAKE BAIKAL

As astonishing as it may seem, there is a single lake that holds more freshwater than the Great Lakes combined. Russia's Lake Baikal is about a third the size of Lake Superior in surface area, but it plunges an amazing 5,315 feet (1,620 meters) deep at its deepest point. Lake Baikal holds over 20 percent of Earth's unfrozen fresh water.

Lake Baikal (above) in Siberia is the deepest lake in the world. Ice covers much of its surface in winter.

Importance

The Great Lakes form North America's most important inland **waterway.** Some ports on the Great Lakes lie over 1,000 miles (1,600 kilometers) from the ocean. Yet ships can sail from these ports to any other port in the world. The ships can reach the Atlantic Ocean with the help of a system of **locks** and **canals** built by the United States and Canada. The locks and canals help ships travel between the lakes, which differ in elevation, or height, above sea level.

One set of canals and locks is the St. Lawrence Seaway. It extends about 450 miles (720 kilometers) from Montreal to the eastern end of Lake Erie. Another set of canals and locks is the Soo Canals. They are on the St. Marys River, which connects Lake Superior and Lake Huron. The Soo Canals and the St. Lawrence Seaway are among the busiest canal systems in the world.

Shipping on the Great Lakes helped to turn the surrounding region into a great industrial area. A vast steel industry once thrived around the Great Lakes. Ships carried iron ore from ports in the U.S. states of Minnesota, Wisconsin, and Michigan to steelmaking centers in the states of Indiana, Ohio, and Pennsylvania. The Great Lakes are also the best way to ship the huge wheat crops of western Canada and the northern United States to milling centers in eastern Canada and in Buffalo, New York. Other ships carry coal, copper, flour, and manufactured goods on the lakes.

A freighter moves slowly across Lake Huron. Each year, thousands of freighters carry iron ore, grain, coal, and other goods across the Great Lakes.

TROUBLED WATERS

As industries and large cities grew up around the Great Lakes, much of the lakes' waters became heavily **polluted.** Efforts have been made to reduce pollution. But **invasive species** remain a problem. Invasive species that have damaged or threatened the Great Lakes include the sea lamprey, zebra mussel, and Asian carp.

The zebra mussel, a freshwater shellfish native to European lakes, has invaded the Great Lakes, where it now occurs in great numbers. The crushed shells of millions of dead zebra mussels (above) accumulate in large piles along the shore of Lake Ontario.

Niagara Falls

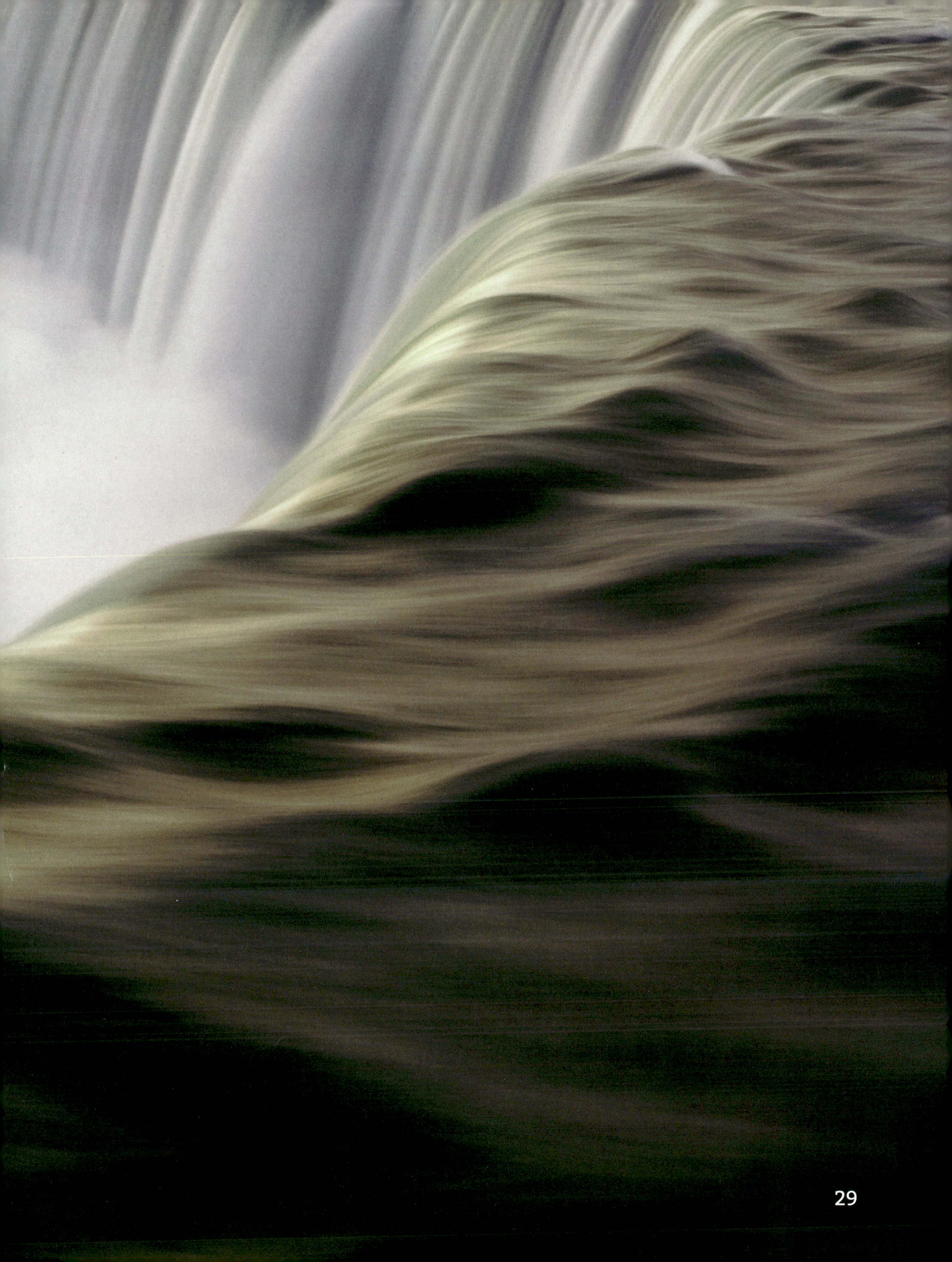

Where Is Niagara Falls and What's Special About It?

Within the Great Lakes system is another wonder of water that is a natural marvel in its own right. Niagara Falls is on the Niagara River, about halfway between Lake Erie and Lake Ontario on the border between the United States and Canada. At the falls, the Niagara River plunges about 170 feet (50 meters) into a steep, canyonlike gorge.

Niagara Falls actually consists of two waterfalls, the Horseshoe Falls and the American Falls. The Horseshoe Falls is on the Canadian side of the border in the province of Ontario. The American Falls is on the United States side in the state of New York. American Falls is slightly taller, but Horseshoe Falls is much larger, carrying some 85 percent of the falls' total water.

The falls have become a popular destination for sightseers and honeymooning couples. Millions of people visit Niagara Falls each year. At night, wide beams of colored lights illuminate the falls. Over the years, more than a dozen daredevils have risked their lives going over the falls in barrels or other contraptions.

A view of the scenic American Falls on the Niagara River from the air (right)

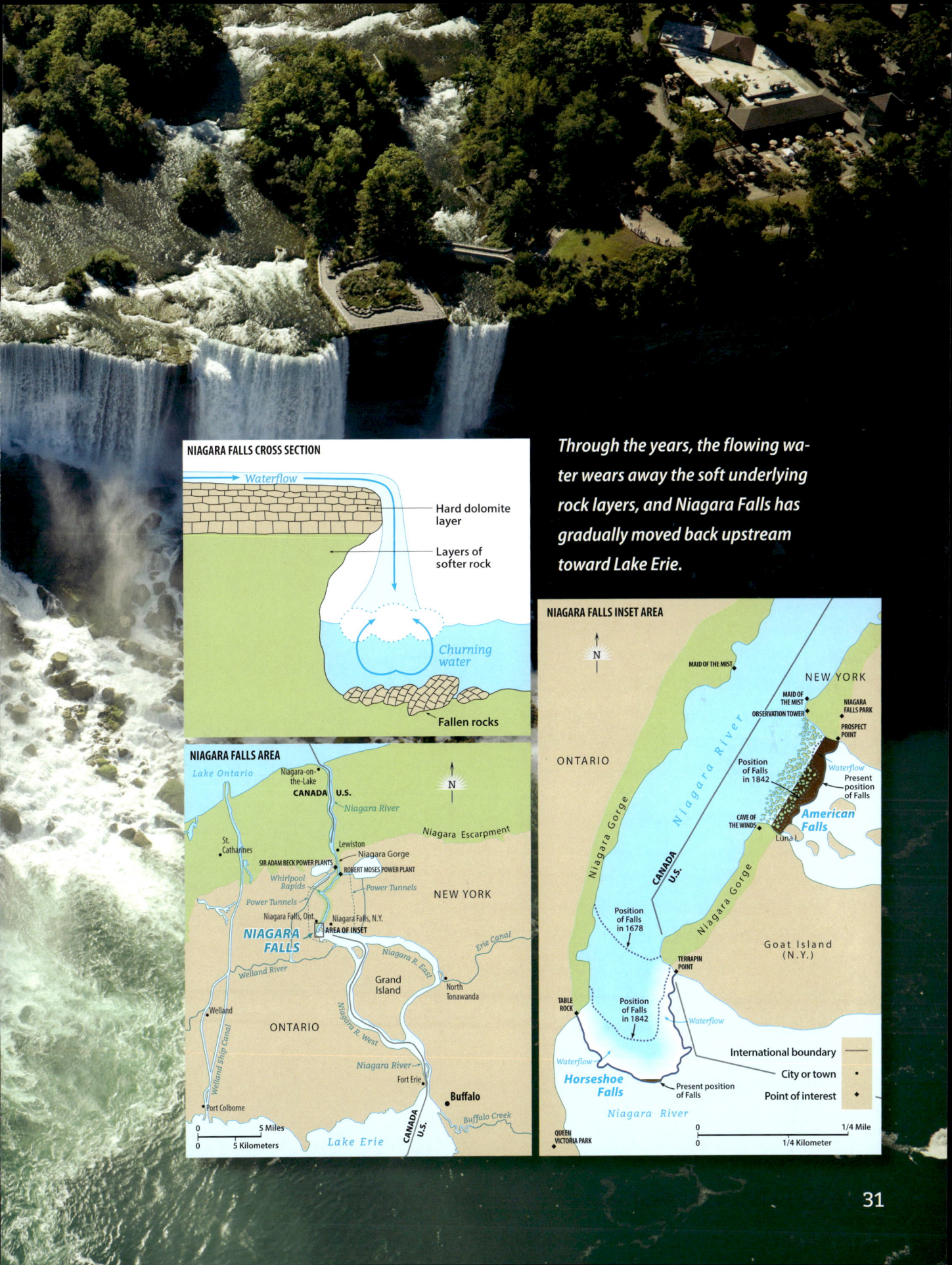

NIAGARA FALLS CROSS SECTION

- Waterflow
- Hard dolomite layer
- Layers of softer rock
- Churning water
- Fallen rocks

Through the years, the flowing water wears away the soft underlying rock layers, and Niagara Falls has gradually moved back upstream toward Lake Erie.

NIAGARA FALLS AREA

Lake Ontario • Niagara-on-the-Lake • CANADA / U.S. • Niagara River • St. Catharines • Lewiston • Niagara Gorge • Niagara Escarpment • SIR ADAM BECK POWER PLANTS • ROBERT MOSES POWER PLANT • Whirlpool Rapids • Power Tunnels • Niagara Falls, Ont. • Niagara Falls, N.Y. • AREA OF INSET • NIAGARA FALLS • NEW YORK • Erie Canal • Welland River • Niagara R. East • Grand Island • North Tonawanda • Welland • Niagara R. West • ONTARIO • Niagara River • Fort Erie • Buffalo • Port Colborne • CANADA / U.S. • Buffalo Creek • Lake Erie • Welland Ship Canal

0   5 Miles
0   5 Kilometers

NIAGARA FALLS INSET AREA

ONTARIO • MAID OF THE MIST • MAID OF THE MIST • OBSERVATION TOWER • NIAGARA FALLS PARK • PROSPECT POINT • NEW YORK • Niagara River • Position of Falls in 1842 • Waterflow • Present position of Falls • CAVE OF THE WINDS • American Falls • Luna I. • Niagara Gorge • CANADA / U.S. • Position of Falls in 1678 • Goat Island (N.Y.) • TERRAPIN POINT • TABLE ROCK • Position of Falls in 1842 • Waterflow • Horseshoe Falls • Present position of Falls • Niagara River • QUEEN VICTORIA PARK

- International boundary
- City or town
- Point of interest

0   1/4 Mile
0   1/4 Kilometer

31

How Niagara Falls Formed

Niagara Falls probably formed about 12,000 years ago. At that time, the last of the huge **glaciers** melted from the Great Lakes region. The melting ice caused Lake Erie to overflow, forming the Niagara River. The river ran northward over a high cliff called the Niagara Escarpment. The river cut through the escarpment and, over the centuries, formed Niagara Falls.

The river and the falls continue to wear away at the underlying rock. This rock consists of many layers. The top layer is about 80 feet (24 meters) thick and consists of a hard rock called dolomite. It covers softer layers of limestone, sandstone, and shale. Water *erodes* (wears away) soft stone faster than hard stone. For this reason, the pounding waters cut deeply into the lower layers, leaving an overhanging ledge of harder rock. Beneath American Falls, for example, the waters have carved a hollow known as the Cave of the Winds.

As the falls carve deeper into the soft layers, the ledge above eventually collapses. As a result, Niagara Falls is moving slowly upstream! The falls were originally near present-day Lewiston, New York. Now they lie about 7 miles (11 kilometers) closer to Lake Erie. The ledge of the Horseshoe Falls wears away at a rate varying from about 3 inches (8 centimeters) to as much as 6 feet (2 meters) per year. The ledge of the American Falls erodes more slowly because less water flows over it. Each year, about 1 inch (2.5 centimeters) wears away.

A continuous cloud of spray rises from the water crashing down at Niagara Falls.

VICTORIA FALLS

On the Zambezi River between the countries of Zambia and Zimbabwe in Southern Africa lies a waterfall about twice as tall as Niagara Falls. Victoria Falls reaches a height of about 355 feet (108 meters) in its center. The mist and spray created by the falls can be seen for a great distance. This cloud and the constant roar of the water caused the people of the area to name the falls *Mosi-oa-Tunya* (smoke that thunders).

A rainbow (above) shines above the mist at Victoria Falls in Africa.

Niagara Falls Attractions

Rainbow Bridge
This bridge spans the Niagara River, connecting the American and Canadian sides.

Maid of the Mist
Several steamers called the Maid of the Mist take sightseers close to the churning waters at the base of the falls.

The American Falls
The American Falls is on the United States side in the state of New York. At night, wide beams of colored lights illuminate the falls.

34

Niagara Falls attracts visitors throughout the year. Parks line both sides of the river near Niagara Falls, with features that provide excellent views.

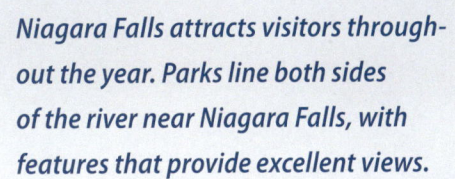

Observation tower
Niagara Falls has four observation towers, ranging from 282 to 500 feet (86 to 150 meters) high, to provide fine views of the falls.

United States
Canada

Horseshoe Falls
The Horseshoe Falls, on the Canadian side of the border, is the largest waterfall at Niagara Falls.

Tourism

Large numbers of tourists first began visiting Niagara Falls during the 1800's. Many hotels and taverns were built on both sides of the falls. In addition, numerous industries began to operate along the Niagara River. Some people believed that the rapid development of tourism and industry ruined the scenic beauty of the Niagara Falls area.

In 1885, the government of the state of New York took control of the land bordering the American Falls. It established Niagara Falls Park, covering about 430 acres (174 hectares), on the land. In 1886, Canada established Queen Victoria Park on 196 acres (79 hectares) of land near the Horseshoe Falls. Since the 1880's, much more land in the Niagara Falls area has been set aside for parks, especially on the Canadian side.

Niagara Falls attracts visitors throughout the year. However, most visitors come during the tourist season, from April 1 to October 31. Excellent views of the falls may be seen from such sites as Prospect Point, Table Rock, and Terrapin Point. Four observation towers, ranging from 282 to 500 feet (86 to 150 meters) high, also provide fine views of the falls. Several steamers that share the name Maid of the Mist take sightseers close to the churning waters at the base of the falls.

A rainbow shines over the Maid of the Mist, which takes tourists right up to the base of Niagara Falls.

GOING OVER THE FALLS

Despite the fact that it is both illegal and highly dangerous, more than a dozen daredevils have sought fame by braving a plunge over Niagara Falls, usually in a barrel or other protective contraption. In 1901, Annie Edson Taylor went over the falls in a barrel, becoming the first recorded person to survive the attempt. Several people have been injured or drowned in the attempt.

Annie Edson Taylor (above) poses with the large barrel inside which she rode over Niagara Falls.

37

Glossary

basin a low region drained by a river and the streams that flow into it

canal an artificial waterway dug across land

delta a low plain of silt, sand, and clay deposited at the mouth of a river

glacier a flowing mass of ice

Himalaya the highest mountain system in the world, located in Asia

invasive species a living thing that spreads outside its natural range, causing problems for people and wildlife native to the habitat

lock a device used to raise or lower ships, allowing them to pass between waterways of different elevation

myth a type of story told to explain the world or its mysteries

pollution waste and other products of human activity that damage the environment

sacred holy, belonging to, or dedicated to God or a god

tectonic plate one of the rigid pieces of rock that make up Earth's outer surface

tributary a stream or river that flows into a larger stream or river

waterway a river, canal, or other body of water on which ships can travel

Find Out More

The Ganges: India's Sacred River (Rivers Around the World) by Molly Aloian (Crabtree Publishing Company, 2010). *Learn facts about the Ganges River and the treasures on its river banks.*

Over the Edge: A Kid's Guide to Niagara Falls, Ontario, Canada by Penelope Dyan and John Weigand (Bellissima Publishing, 2010). *Readers will learn about Niagara Falls and the area's fun activities.*

The Mystery on the Great Lakes: Michigan, Superior, Huron, Ontario, Erie (Real Kids, Real Places) by Carole Marsh (Gallopade International, 2010). *This book reads like a mystery, but it is full of facts and vocabulary words that will teach readers more about the Great Lakes.*

Use Your Noodle!

Being fabled can be both a blessing and a curse. What are some of the problems faced by the waters in this book? How many of them are caused by people? What are some ways to protect these waters for future generations?

Acknowledgments

Cover	© Jay Kerr, Shutterstock
4-5	© iStock
6-7	© iStock
8-9	© iStock
10-11	© Phuong D. Nguyen, Shutterstock; The God Khnum (1823), colour lithograph by Jean Francois Champollion; Archives Charmet (Bridgeman Images)
12-13	© Frank Bienewal, Alamy Images; © Dennis Cox, Alamy Images
14-15	© Tatiana Dyuvbanova, Shutterstock
16-17	© David Pearson, Alamy Images; © Shutterstock
18-19	© Shutterstock; © Shutterstock; © Kevin Schafer, Alamy Images; © Roland Seitre, Minden Pictures/SuperStock; © Stuart Forster, Alamy Images
20-21	Jeff Schmaltz, NASA/MODIS Rapid Response Team/Goddard Space Flight Center
22-23	© iStock
24-25	© Don Johnston, Alamy Images; © Tuul and Bruno Morandi, Alamy Images
26-27	© Mark Scheuern, Alamy Images; © All Canada Photos/Alamy Images
28-29	© Jay Kerr, Shutterstock
30-31	© iStock
32-33	© iStock; © Henk Ruitenbeek, iStock
34-35	© Ritu Manoj Jethani, Shutterstock; © Sol 90 Images
36-37	© iStock; Library of Congress

Index

A
aarti ritual, 16, 17
American Falls, 30-32, 34, 36; map, 31
animals, 18-19
Asia, 14

B
Bangladesh, 12
basins, 4, 12, 14
Brahma, 10
Brahmaputra River, 8, 12

C
Canada, and Niagara Falls, 4, 22, 26, 30, 35, 36
canals, 26
Cave of the Winds, 32
China, 13

D
deer, barasingha, 18
dolomite, 32
dolphins, Ganges river, 19

E
Earth: Ganges and, 10; water on, 4. *See also* tectonic plates
Egyptians, ancient, 11
erosion, of Niagara Falls, 31, 32

G
Ganga, 10
Ganges, 4, 6-19; features of, 8-9, 12; formation of, 14-15; Hindu religion and, 8, 10-11, 16-17; maps, 5, 9; tributaries of, 12, 14, 18; wildlife of, 18-19
Ganges Delta, 12, 14, 19
Gangetic basin, 14
Gangotri Glacier, 12-13
Gaumakh cave, 12
gavials, 18
glaciers, 12-13, 24, 32
Great Lakes, 4, 20-27, 30; features of, 22; formation of, 24-25; importance as waterway, 26; maps, 5, 23; problems with, 27

H
Himalaya, 4, 8, 12, 14, 18
Hindu religion, 8, 10-11, 16-17
Horseshoe Falls, 30, 32, 35, 36; map, 31

I
India, 4, 8; course of Ganges in, 12; Ganges formation in, 14; Hindu religion in, 8, 10-11, 16-17
invasive species, 27

J
junks, 13

K
Khnum, 11
Kumbh Mela festival, 16-17

L
Lake Baikal, 25
Lake Erie, 4, 22, 30, 32; map, 23
Lake Huron, 4, 22, 26-27; map, 23
Lake Michigan, 4, 22-23; map, 23
Lake Ontario, 4, 22, 30; map, 23
Lake Superior, 4, 22, 24-26; map, 23
landforms, 5
locks (shipping), 26

M
Maid of the Mist, 34, 36
mangroves, 19
moksha, 16
monkeys, rhesus, 19
mussels, zebra, 27
myth, 10

N
New York (state), 30, 32, 34, 36
Niagara Escarpment, 32
Niagara Falls, 4, 28-37; attractions, 34-35; features of, 30-31; formation of, 32; going over, 30, 37; maps, 5, 31; tourism, 30, 36-37
Niagara Falls Park, 36
Niagara River, 30-32, 36
Nile, 11

P
Padma River, 12
pilgrims, Hindu, 12-13, 16
pollution, 18, 27

Q
Queen Victoria Park, 36

R
Rainbow Bridge, 34
Russia, 25

S
sacred rivers, 4, 8, 10-11, 16-17
Sagara, King, 10
St. Lawrence Seaway, 26
sharks, Ganges, 19
shipping, 26
Shiva, 10
silt, 14
snow leopards, 18
Soo Canals, 26
steel industry, 26
Sundarbans, 19

T
Taylor, Annie Edson, 37
tectonic plates, 14
tourism, 30, 36-37

U
United States, and Niagara Falls, 4, 22, 26, 30, 34, 36

V
Varanasi, India, 10-11, 16-17
Victoria Falls, 33
Vishnu, 10

W
water, fresh, 4, 22
waterways, 8, 26

Y
Yangtze River, 13

Z
Zambezi River, 33